A Glorious Anniversary
Celebrating 90 Years of Ministry
1925 to 2016

Assyrian Presbyterian Church
Turlock, California

Glorious Anniversary—Celebrating 90 years of Ministry, 1925-2016—Assyrian Presbyterian Church, Turlock, California

Copyright © 2018 by Julius W. Mirza

Credits:

Julius W. Mirza, Compiler and Editor
James A. Tweedie, Assistant Editor

All rights reserved. No part of this book may be reproduced or transmitted in any form or by any means without written permission from the author.

Printed in USA by Dunecrest Press, Long Beach, WA 98631

ISBN   978-1-945539-19-0
LCCN   2018946982

Table of Contents

Acknowledgements	1
Glorious Anniversary	4
Thanks from Turlock Historical Society	8
Welcome from Monica Boehme	11
Remarks by Mrs. Thea Harris	12
Remarks by Milton David, M.D.	13
Remarks by Eleanor Jean Huskins	14
Remarks of the Rev. Edward William Eissabake	17
Brief Biographies of Elisha and Victoria David	30
Pastor Biography—Rev. Dr. Elisha David	36
Pastor Biography—Rev. Stephen O. Khoobyar	47
Pastor Biography—Rev. Darius Baba Yohannan	58
Pastor Biography—Rev. Dr. George Shahbaz	67
Pastor Biography—Rev. Edward William Eissabake	75
Appendix—Celebration Documents	85

Acknowledgements

This memory book not only celebrates the 90th anniversary of the founding of St. John's Assyrian Presbyterian Church, but also recounts a brief history of how the Assyrian community in Turlock foresaw their dreams of acquiring their own church to celebrate their Christian faith spoken in the Assyrian language

After attending the successful historical 90th anniversary commemorating the existence of St. John's, my heart implored me to approach Milton David, M.D., Pastor Edward Eissabake and Sargon Eddy about documenting this historic occasion in the life of the church. My function, as Julius W. (Jay) Mirza, is not to act as the author, but chronicler and assembler of historic data to tell the story of St. John's.

I am most grateful to and acknowledge with genuine sincerity the following persons for their assistance:

Pastor Edward William Eissabake

Pastor Edward patiently shepherded me through all the persons that were involved in the collection of historical data from 1925 until 2003. He provided me with newspaper articles, important letters in the outreach of the Assyrian community in Turlock to attract an Assyrian-speaking pastor and the financial wherewithal to build the church. In addition, he gave me computer files and photographs. Last but not least, he wrote his personal biography

Mr. Sargon Eddy, Elder

As Elder, Sargon was the perfect resource to lead me to the proper persons in the church community. Contact lists along with phone numbers and e-mail addresses opened many doors

Turlock Historical Society

Mrs. Monica Boehme, past President and Thea Harris, President of the Turlock Historical Society in 2016 were extremely helpful in leading me to persons most directly related to the Society's efforts to successfully carry out the program called

"How Turlock became the City of Churches"

Milton C. David, M.D. & Eleanor David Huskins

Milton and Eleanor, children of the of the late Rev. Dr. Elisha David, first pastor of St. John's Assyrian Presbyterian Church in Turlock, ministering from 1925 to 1954. Milton and Eleanor contributed to the biography of their father Elisha and mother Victoria. Milton worked closely with Monica Boehme of the Turlock Historical Society in the preparations of "How Turlock became the city of Churches" featuring St. John's Assyrian Presbyterian Church as the second Turlock church in the publication, Turlock Historical Record, beginning in 2015

Milton (Milt) Khoobyarian

After 27 years, it was sheer joy when I discovered where Milt and his wife Joanne were living. They reside in a retirement center in Los Gatos, CA. I was pleased to find out that Milt had written a very complete biography of his parents entitled:

"The lives of Stephen and Piour Khoobyar"

It is with Milt's permission that he has permitted me to summarize some of the late Rev. Stephen O. Khoobyar's biography, ISBN 0-9729597- 0 -1

Nancy S. Yohannan

Nancy was most helpful in gathering and coordinating the information on the biography of her parents, Pastor Darius Yohannan and his wife Lily. She verified the accuracy of their biography with the input that I gathered from the history of the pastors ministering at St. John's Assyrian Presbyterian Church

Reverend Dr. George Shahbaz

Pastor George was the fourth (4th) pastor in succession ministering to the church congregation in Turlock. Since George is currently pastor of the United Assyrian Evangelical Church, I interviewed him and his wife Amal, for their biography

March 11, 1932
Dedication of Stained Glass window
Christ praying in Gethsemane Garden
In memory of
Rev. William Ambrose Shedd, D.D.
And his wife, Louise Wilbur Shedd
Who died in Persia

Glorious Anniversary

Celebrating 90 years of Worship in Turlock
St. John's Assyrian Presbyterian Church
August 02, 2016

Unfortunately, history has a tendency to repeat itself. It is ironic that Assyrian are being persecuted in the Middle East today because of their Christian beliefs. This inhuman tragedy began in northwestern Iran during WW1, 1914 –1918. Assyrians were driven away from their villages and killed by Turks, Kurds and Iranians.

Thus began the exodus of Christian Assyrians to Russia, America and many other countries for their safety and survival. They were committed to practice their Christian faith. It is reported that the Rev. Dr. Isaac Adams family were the first Assyrians to establish their home in the Turlock / Livingston area in 1911.

The Reverend Dr. Isaac Adams & Family—1928
Back row: Clarence, Arthur, Clara, Albert, & John Calvin Adams
Middle row: Sarah, Florence, Edward, Dr. Isaac Adams & Henry Herman Adams

In 1915, the estimated population of Turlock was about 1500. By now, there were 10 Assyrian families established in this small community. By 1921, the Assyrian community had grown to 200 residents. This fact was published on May 14, 1920 in the *Turlock Daily Journal* entitled "Assyrian refugees, persecuted by the Turks, are coming to Turlock." On November 10, 1925, four leaders of the Assyrian community (Rev. David Joseph, K.H. Shimmon, Lazar Pera and George Petros) who had been meeting in an old wood frame building for church, extended a written invitation to Rev. Dr. Elisha David to organize an Assyrian Presbyterian Congregation. The Presbyterian preference was requested because most of the 10 families were of the Presbyterian denomination before immigrating to America. Rev. Elisha David was a graduate of Dubuque University and seminary in Dubuque, Iowa.

Initially, the Assyrians met in the Swedish Tabernacle. For financial assistance in establishing the first Assyrian church in Turlock, Board of National Missions – San Francisco, Board of National Missions, New York and the Fourth Presbyterian Church in Chicago were contacted. Under the guidance of the Presbytery of San Joaquin, the first Assyrian Presbyterian Church was established in Turlock on January 13, 1926 with some 60 members.

With Presbytery assistance, architect Rollin S. Tuttle of Oakland was retained to design the new church. The property was located at 450 S. Palm Street and was purchased from the City of Turlock for $1,000. Construction of the Spanish Style church by Thomas A. Cuthberston of San Francisco was completed on November 27, 1927 for $21,000. The Church was dedicated on December 16, 1928 by the late Rev. Walter E. Edmunds of the Synod of California, in Glendale.

The church was serving San Francisco and Turlock colonies of Assyrians. Donations for constructing this church came from church members of the Assyrian community and American friends in the United States, primarily from San Francisco, New York and Chicago.

The Presbyterian preference was requested because most of the 10 families were of the Presbyterian denomination before immigrating to America.

Initially, the Assyrians met in the Swedish Tabernacle. For financial assistance in establishing the first Assyrian church in Turlock, Board of National Missions – San

Turlock, California.
Nov. 10, 1925.

Rev. John Timothy Stone, D.D.
Chicago, Illinois.

Dear Sir:

Though I met you once in San Francisco during the War time, I know you more through our people in Chicago as American People call George Washington, the Father of their Country, also our Assyrian People call you their Father for if it wasn't through your kindness and help, Rev. Ahlahal or our Church would be a very little known about. We are waiting to see Mr. Elisha David to accept our call and help us to build a church for our people in Turlock. Mr. Elisha and I both were friends and just like brothers since our childhood. I do not need to tell you more about him for I am sure you know him more than what I know.

Last Sunday we had a good meeting and did our very best to raise money for Mr. Elisha's call. All our people suffered this year. The loss was heavy in grapes, etc, so my heart is beating to hear if my beloved Elisha David will accept our call. We are struggling for a good minister to come and help us. I am sure Mr. David is the man we need. Our future is very bright. We hope within a few years that we will have the biggest church in the West.

To close, it is my desire and Prayer that may GOD, through our Christian Brethern, fulfill our Great need.

Very truly yours,

George Peter

Francisco, Board of National Missions - New York and the Fourth Presbyterian Church in Chicago were contacted. Under the guidance of the Presbytery of San Joaquin (Stockton, CA), the first Assyrian Presbyterian Church was established in Turlock on January 13, 1926 with some 60 members.

The church was serving San Francisco and Turlock colonies of Assyrians. Donations for constructing this church came from church members of the Assyrian community and American friends in United States, primarily from California, New York and Chicago.

In 1958, after joining the Presbyterian Church (USA), and United Presbyterian Church of Northern America, the name of the church was changed to St. John's Assyrian United Presbyterian Church.

In 1983, after joining the United Presbyterian Church and Presbyterian Church (USA), the name of the church was changed to St. John's Assyrian Presbyterian Church (PCUSA).

St. John's was a member of the Sierra Mission Partnership and the Stockton Presbytery until 2014 when St. John's Assyrian PCUSA unanimously voted to join the Evangelical Presbyterian Church (EPC) denomination.

Pastors of St. John's Assyrian EPC

1925 – 1954	Rev. Dr. Elisha David (D.D.)
1956 – 1961	Rev. Stephen O. Khoobyar
1963 – 1983	Rev. Darius B. Yohannan
1983 – 2003	Rev. Dr. George Shahbaz
2003 – today	Rev. Edward William Eissabake

Interim Pastors and Associate Pastors
Stockton Presbytery Interim Pastors

Rev. Dr. Harberts;
Rev. Frank Humberger;
Rev. Lee Heim

Assistant Pastors

The late Rev. J. Prichard Amstus;
Dr. Dan Erickson (People Matter Ministries-Montana);
Rev. Dr. Jon Venema (Senior Pastor of Grace Community Church, Visalia, CA)

Evolution of Church Name Changes

November 27, 1955, the Church adopted the name of
St. John's Assyrian Presbyterian Church

Thanks from the Turlock Historical Society

Every year it is our plan to highlight one of Turlock's churches. We originally came up with the idea for this series because in 1932 Robert Ripley a cartoonist known nationally for Ripley's "Believe It or Not," called our town "The City of Churches." The town at the time had more churches per capita than any other city in the United States. Many of Turlock's churches were established pre WW1. Churches were based on ethnic, cultural and language backgrounds. But many early churches supported each other and held functions together. In later years following WW1 more and more churches were established which reflects the growing diverse population of the town during the era between the wars.

Thank you to Dr. Milton David, this event could not have taken place without your initial contact with the Turlock Historical Society and your willingness to share your family history. Your faith and support of the church is admirable. Thank you also to Rev. Edward Eissabake and Mr. Sargon Eddy for your excitement and hard work that made this event so meaningful and successful

The 90th Year of Celebration

About two weeks before the celebration, it was announced at Turlock churches that St. John's Assyrian Presbyterian Church was going to celebrate this most significant anniversary on August 02, 2016 at 6:30 pm in St. John's main sanctuary.

As the title implied by Mr. Ripley in the 1930s, he called Turlock "The City of Churches." The town at the time had more churches per capita than any other city in the United States. With the explosion of immigrants from many parts of the world to Turlock, this announcement created an immense interest in the community.

As the visitors and church members began to fill the pews, it became obvious that the audience was a mixture of Assyrians and other ethnic groups. Looking around the church I recognized many friends. There was an air of anticipation prevalent in the audience. With the overflow of interested persons, folding chairs were placed in the aisles. One could feel the excitement building to a crescendo as the hour for the celebration approached.

There were reserved seats in the front pews of the sanctuary for church members and guests of honor, Dwight Elisha David (deceased) Milton Curtis David and Eleanor David Huskins, children of the late Rev. Dr. Elisha David.

It was at this moment that Milton and Eleanor felt so proud and humble to be recognized by the church as children of Pastor Elisha David and their mother Victoria. Coming firsthand from Pastor Edward Eissabake, praising the tremendous achievements accomplished in forming a new church and successfully locating the funds to build the house of worship. In addition when one considers the diaspora of the new members, Pastor Elisha earned their respect as their new Pastor. His goal from day one was to stress the importance to the members that they were worshipping God in an American Presbyterian Church.

From their childhood days, Pastor Elisha David explained to his children that the two main reasons why Assyrian farmers came to Turlock from Iran was: (1) the latitude of Turlock, (34 degrees north of the equator) was the same as Lake Urmia where grapes have grown for hundreds of years. (2) The availability of water to irrigate grapes was the most crucial reason why the Assyrians settled in the Turlock area. In the late 1800s the Turlock Irrigation District had dammed the Tuolumne River at La Grange and built canals to transport the water to farms in Stanislaus County.

The opening of the celebration began with a welcome statement from Monica Boehme, on behalf of the Turlock Historical Society. This was followed by remarks from Thea Harris, 2016 President of the Turlock Historical Society.

Monica Boehme—Turlock Historical Society
welcoming the audience

Welcome From Monica Boehme

Hello, welcome to the 2nd installation of our series: "How Turlock became known as the city of churches." My name is Monica Boehme, and I am excited to welcome you on behalf of the Turlock Historical Society to St. John's Assyrian Presbyterian Church.

We originally came up with the idea for this series because in 1932 Robert Ripley a cartoonist known nationally for Ripley's "Believe It or Not," called our town "The City of Churches." The town at the time had more churches per capita than any other town in the United States. Many of Turlock's churches were established pre WW1. Churches were established based on ethnic, cultural and language backgrounds. But many early churches supported each other and had functions together. In Later years following WW1 more and more churches were established which reflects the growing diverse population of the town during the era between the wars.

Every year it is our plan to highlight one of Turlock's churches. Tonight we are here to learn about St. John's Assyrian Presbyterian Church. It is our hope that tonight we share with you the history of the church from many aspects: personal history, architectural history, congregational history, cultural changes, community life and others.

But before we begin I would like to welcome Mrs. Thea Harris. She is our Museum Coordinator. She is going to talk with you shortly about the Turlock Historical Society and our museum. About how it began and the goals we have for the future.

In closing, I need your help to thank some special people that have made tonight possible. First Dr. Milton David, thank you so much. He really is the one responsible for tonight as he is the one that reached out to me about his father's church. He has been willing to share his family history in such a special and meaningful way. His passion and wealth of knowledge for the history of this church and the Assyrian people is inspiring.

Thank you to Mr. Sargon Eddy for all your hard work and enthusiasm culminating in tonight's celebration. Your church is lucky to have you and your heart in this community.

Thank you to Khasha Edward and to the entire church community for opening your doors and hearts to share with us tonight. Because of you and Mr. Eddy, we are able to see and experience the living history of St John's Assyrian Presbyterian Church and our town through the years into the present. So, thank you so much for inviting us and for all your hard work.

After the celebration, we invite you to share in some time of fellowship and refreshments provided by the St. John's Assyrian Presbyterian Church Ladies group in the social hall. Thank you all for coming.

Remarks by Mrs. Thea Harris
2016 President of the Turlock Historical Society

We are so pleased to represent the Turlock Historical Society on this very auspicious occasion, celebrating your 90th year of Ministry at St. John's Assyrian Presbyterian Church in Turlock.

The Society was organized in 1994 with the original charter board members; Scott Atherton, Chrissie Collins, Darlene Freeman, Diane Miles, Kristen and Robert Santos. Through the years membership has grown to approximately 450. The Board has been expanded to 19 persons. The Society's publications, meetings and the museum, support the Mission Statement: Collect, Chronicle and Preserve Historical data, Verbal Accounts pertaining to the City of Turlock artifacts, for future generations.

The Albert Chatam Building, circa 1911, was donated by William and Ida Mae Ripley Foundation to the Turlock Historical Society in 1999. The Grand Opening for the Museum was held on Saturday August 02, 2003.

The Society is totally supported by private donations and annual membership dues. I encourage you to give generously so that we can continue our efforts to collect and chronicle the history of Turlock.

Thank you for inviting us to this extraordinary celebration.

Remarks by Milton David, M.D.,
Son of the founder of the church, the late Reverend Dr. Elisha David

The family of the Reverend Dr. Elisha David and Victoria are honored to have you attend this 90th celebration of the Assyrian Presbyterian Church in Turlock. I am grateful to the Turlock Historical Society for featuring this church as the second church in their publication " Turlock Historical Record" called "How Turlock became known as the city of churches."

Dr. Milton David addressing the audience

This 90th celebration could not have taken place without the research performed by pastor Edward Eissabake on the history of this church. After the official ceremony, on the walls of the basement social hall you will be most impressed by the historical documentation.

My father, Elisha David, grew up in the village of Seiri, near the city of Urmia, Azerbaijan Province, Iran. This village was higher in elevation than the surrounding Assyrian villages. Today it is the gateway to skiing in the foothills leading to the Zagros Mountains.

In 1833, the American Presbyterian Medical Mission was established in the city of Urmia. This facility provided medical care to the local villages including Seiri. It was at this time that Elisha David met Dr. Shedd and Dr. Cochran who were sponsored by the Fourth Presbyterian Church in Chicago. It was this exposure to doctors in the Christian faith that encouraged Elisha to go to America and study to be a Presbyterian minister.

After completing his elementary and high school education in Seiri, my father met Dr. Timothy Stone, senior pastor in Urmia, who encouraged him to go to America and study at the Dubuque Seminary of the University of Dubuque in Iowa.

He arrived in America at the age of 24 in 1905 and came to Chicago and lived with Dr. Stone's family until he was admitted to Seminary. He graduated from seminary in 1923, at the age of 42. In 1925, at the request of his cousin Geroosha Addy, he came to Turlock to serve the Assyrian community.

Under the guidance of the Presbytery of San Joaquin, the first Assyrian Presbyterian Church in Turlock was established, serving the Turlock and San Francisco communities. The church that you are in today, was completed on 16 December 1928. My father and mother served the church from 1925 to 1954.

Remarks by Eleanor Jean Huskins
Daughter of the founder of the church, the Reverend Dr. Elisha David

My mother, Victoria Esther Adams was born in North Battleford, Saskatchewan, Canada. She met my father, the Reverend Dr. Elisha David, in Turlock in 1925 and they were married on 14 June 1926. I am very proud to show you my mother's wedding gown. I have preserved it as a family heirloom.

My mother supported my father in his role as pastor of the church, teaching Sunday school, active in the Women's Christian Association and the Women's Christian Temperance Society.

She raised three children while she participating in church related activities. As a homemaker, she loved to bake. She won a number of prizes for baking "Upside down Pineapple Cake," in the Stanislaus County Fair in Turlock.

Eleanor Jean Huskins, addressing the audience

Eleanor displaying her mother's wedding dress to the audience

Remarks of the Rev. Edward William Eissabake
Pastor of St. John's Assyrian Presbyterian Church, Turlock, CA

Welcome:

It is such a lovely evening. As we are to grace this occasion. Allow me to welcome each and every one of you to the House of God and to the St. John's Assyrian Evangelical Presbyterian Church of Turlock.

Yours truly, the Rev. Edward William Eissabake, the ordained minister, teaching elder and pastor of this church, would like to thank Turlock Historical Society for recognizing our church as their 2nd annual event of How Turlock Became the City of the Churches!

Pastor Edward Eissabake addressing the audience

The First written prayer of the church on January 13th, 1926

"O God in Thee we trust and we do believe that thou wilt bless our effort in building a church which we have been longing for about six (06) or seven (07) years, that we might worship Thee according to our Holy Doctrine. Thanks be to Thee O God. Thou has heard our prayers, Thou has given us a beloved and sacrificed self, the pastor Rev. Elisha David. We invoke thy blessings O God, that we may be a consecrated and holy church, to go forth gathering sinners in Thy Kingdom, and building saints in Thee. O God, we need a place of worship, wherein we may worship Thee. We trust that Thee will provide for us, in order that we may be more effective in serving Thee and our fellowmen." Amen!

Introducing the History and Ministry of the St. John's Assyrian Evangelical Presbyterian Church

The St. John's Assyrian Evangelical Presbyterian Church is located at 450 South Palm St. Turlock, CA 95380. Currently, the St. John's has three pieces of property as one complex:

1. The Church Building with 6,915 S.F. on a lot size of 19,602 S.F.

2. The Manse (The building in the back of the church building) is used for the educational purposes.

3. The empty small property on the left side of the church

All three pieces of properties are paid off and currently the church does not have any standing loan on the properties.

All the facilities of the St. John's are only for the religious purposes and fall under the Non-profit organization status (501C3).

In 1915, while the total population of Turlock reported being 1,500, there were ten Assyrian families living in Turlock. By 1921, the Assyrian community grew to a degree (200 people). The Assyrians migration to the region was so noticeable that the Turlock Daily Journal published an article titled "Assyrian refugees, persecuted by the Turks, are coming to Turlock" (May 14, 1920). As more Assyrians moved to Turlock, the predominant denomination, Presbyterian, decided to have its own church. On November 10th, 1925 the leaders of the worshiping group in an old wooden house (Rev. David Joseph, K.H. Shimmon, Lazar Pera, and George Petros) officially and in writing extended a call to Rev. Elisha David to organize an Assyrian Presbyterian congregation and to be their pastor. Rev. David came from Dubuque college and seminary in Dubuque, Iowa. Initially, the congregation moved into Swedish Tabernacle, paying rent [1] (*The Watchman, Church Extension Board Bulletin, No. 464- San Francisco, CA, January 1936. (On 10th anniversary of the St. John's EPC*) for the use of it. With the aid of the Board of National Missions-San Francisco (the late Rev. Dr. Philip F. Payne), and the Board of New York, and the support of the 4th Presbyterian Church of Chicago (the late Rev. Dr. Timothy Stone) the Assyrian Presbyterian Church as the first Assyrian Church in Turlock[2] (*Stockton Record (Stockton-San Joaquin County)- Friday December 14th, 1928*), and the only and first Assyrian registered Presbyterian church in California and west of Chicago[3] (*Fresno Bee, Vol. 13, Section-B-No. 2148, December 17th, 1928*) was organized by the Presbytery of San Joaquin with almost 60 members on January 13th, 1926. On November 27th, 1927 the construction of the church building was completed. The church was dedicated on Sunday morning December 16, 1928, by the late Rev. Walter E. Edmunds (from Glendale-Moderator of the Synod of California) (*Turlock Tribune- Volume XIX, No. 139, Friday December 14th, 1928*). The church was serving San Francisco and Turlock colonies of Assyrian people. The total cost of the church building was $21,000.00 [4] (*Modesto Herald News- December 17th, 1928*). It came from the donation of the church members and Assyrian community, American friends in the United States (California, Chicago and New York). The Architect was Rollin S. Tuttle of Oakland, and the builder, Thomas A. Cuthberston from San Francisco. The building is of Spanish type architecture. The land was purchased from the City of Turlock for $1,000.00. On November 27th, 1955, the church adopted the name of the **St. John's** Assyrian Presbyterian Church. In 1958, after joining the Presbyterian USA and United Presbyterian of Northern America, the name of the church was transformed to the St. John's Assyrian **United** Presbyterian Church. In 1983, after joining the United Presbyterian Church and the Presbyterian Church in the U.S., the name of the congregation was called the St. John Assyrian Presbyterian Church **(PCUSA)**. The St. John was a member of the

---

[1] *The Watchman, Church Extension Board Bulletin, No. 464- San Francisco, CA, January 1936. (On 10th anniversary of the St. John's EPC)*
[2] *Stockton Record (Stockton-San Joaquin County)- Friday December 14th, 1928*
[3] *Fresno Bee, Vol. 13, Section-B-No. 2148, December 17th, 1928*
[4] *Modesto Herald News- December 17th, 1928*

Sierra Mission Partnership and the Stockton Presbytery until year 2014 when the St. John's Assyrian PCUSA unanimously voted to join the Evangelical Presbyterian Church *(EPC)* denomination.

Top Four Character Traits of the St. John's

1) Endurance and Perseverance:

- Language
- Ethnicity
- Reformed Theology (not changing the theology and Christian teachings).
- Maintaining the bible principles and standing on those truths.
- Joining California Christian Citizens Association 1960 regarding freedom to read bible in public schools.

2) A Connectional Church

- With denomination
- With our roots in Middle East (window 1932)-
- City of Turlock and State University Stanislaus County 1960 President J. Burton Vasche
- Connected with other churches from different ethnic background: ECC- Active in Counsel of churches in Turlock- Raising Fund to Billy Graham Crusade in 1958.
- Joining Disaster Program of the City of Turlock under the leadership of Lt. Col. George F. Tarr.
- Joining Civic Club and other two churches (Evangelical Church and Church of the East) for having cooperative events.
- Assyrian in other states: Sending articles to Assyrian Star Magazine (Late Rev. Joel Varda)- Connecting to Assyrian Federation Community (not a member- but friends)

3) Sharing, Caring, Inclusiveness:

- To Japanese after the Pearl Harbor 1942 (maintaining the belongings)
- sending financial supports to Tabriz Hospital, To blind children in Iran, to boys school in Iran, sending 332 ib clothes to Middle East in 1967. There was a und in helping Assyrians called, " 50 million fund drive!"

- Sending boxes of candies and cookies to Assyrian soldiers in service regardless of their denomination.
- Helping Hungarians in 1956
- Serving Laotian community (monthly feeding and Christmas gifts up to 100 children in Turlock).
- Supporting a missionary by name Kenny Joseph to Japan
- Supporting disasters

4) **Visioning for Future:**

- Welcoming ministry of Mariners
- Having at least 3 English speaking assistant pastors
- Believe in Unity and not supporting divisions
- Teaching Assyrian Language and Christian Teachings (The most successful Assyrian VBS)

Current Status

- Pastor Edward is the 5th pastor of the church…he is the only employee of the church.
- Sunday service at 11:00am.
- Session: eight elder
- Deacons: eight deacons
- Almost 210 members, but 170 active members…
- FSM: Facility Services Management
- Having two congregational meetings:
- December: Election of the Officers
- January: Annual Reports and Approving the Annual Budget

Ministries

- Sunday school- 12-15 students. VBS in the month of June 55 children plus 35 teachers and helpers (year 2015)
- Bible Studies: 30-40 attendees
- Women's Bible Study: Book of Revelation (2015)
- Youth Group: 12 students (2016)
- Choir: (12-18 singers)

- ❖ Women's Ministry
- ❖ Homeless Feeding (once a month)
- ❖ Membership Orientation: Four (04) times a year
- ❖ Leadership Training: I know My Church: 20 of the leaders received 12 hours of training.
- ❖ Membership Training: "I Know My Church."

Other

- ❖ Fundraising and Working on Awareness of the Assyrians in the Middle East
- ❖ Praying and seeking a Christian Educator
- ❖ Some special services we hold:
- ❖ Christmas Caroling
- ❖ Remembering our water baptism - on Baptism of the Lord Sunday
- ❖ World Day of Prayer (by women)
- ❖ Ascension of the Lord (full service and traditional rice pudding gathering + wearing white clothes)
- ❖ Reformation Sunday and Presbyterian Heritage Sunday
- ❖ Fall Festival Outreach (Assyrian Food Festival)
- ❖ Thanksgiving Concert
- ❖ Youth Sunday in August
- ❖ Observing Assyrian Martyr Day
- ❖ Monthly women special gatherings
- ❖ Christmas Gifts for Homeless People of the Community.

Challenges

In House:

- ❖ Resources: (personnel, skills, financial, variety of ministries)
- ❖ Space: (Geography of our church-age, size)
- ❖ Language: (having four (4) different languages: Assyrian, Farsi, Arabic, English)
- ❖ The younger generation is more inclined to speak English and be more comfortable in an English-speaking congregation.

- ❖ Need for having a second service in English.
- ❖ Limited Trained Ministers - Pastor as a multipurpose educator
- ❖ Limited Financial Resources
- ❖ Need for developing and improving in evangelism… (not a very hot congregation for mission and evangelism)
- ❖ Excited Christians but need for more Christian maturity, especially among the leaders.
- ❖ Not having an active office due to financial challenges.
- ❖ Having one worship service (traditional and contemporary worships are mixed and create some tension in some areas).
- ❖ Building and facility limitation, for holding different ministries (limited space and facilities for children especially).

Within Community

- ❖ Limited Financial Resources
- ❖ Labeling Presbyterians wrongfully
- ❖ Assyrian and Crisis in Middle East and Anger, hatred and nationalism movement and its impact on the church…
- ❖ Need for UNITY among the Assyrian congregations.
- ❖ Challenges from the Assyrian Ancient church and treating Presbyterians as betrayals and … pushing the notion of Mother Church…

What to Celebrate:

- ❖ 90⁺ anniversary of life in the congregation.
- ❖ People come to Christ regularly.
- ❖ People heal from their sicknesses…
- ❖ The Gospel and the Word of God is preached and taught profoundly
- ❖ Power of prayer is obvious in all the levels of ministry of the church
- ❖ St. John's Church has become a Lighthouse for many…
- ❖ Many membership transfers from different denominations.
- ❖ A peaceful and accepting spirit in almost all the areas toward a constructive change…
- ❖ Not having much gossip among our members…
- ❖ Having a respectful and influential ministry among the Assyrian protestant denominations in California.

Closing:

They carefully followed the true doctrine, manner of life, purpose, faith, longsuffering, love, perseverance, accepted persecutions, afflictions, which happened to them.

Usually, old people are alone… we are not alone, but we like to have more friends…friends like you! We started with friends…we continued with friends and we want to be with friends in our old age…

The meaning of life and ministry was to give life and ministry meaning…they gave meaning to all most everything and they meant what they did.

The tragedy of life is not that it gets old or ends so soon, but that we wait so long to begin it… we are old, but we have started to live again…

We are old but never too old to set another goal or to dream a new dream…

Winston Churchill said, "We make a living by what we get, we make a life by what we give…"

They gave all…they gave life…

Be a friend a fill one of the cards in the pews…

Pastor Edward Eissabake receiving a plaque from Mr. Sam David, President of the Assyrian American Civic Club of Turlock commemorating 90 years of Christian Ministry to the Assyrian population in Turlock

Pastor Elisha Agassi, Elder Ramil Yaldaei Milton David, Eleanor Huskins, Carol David

Candle lighting by Pastor Eissabake and Nancy Yohannan

Elder Sargon Eddy, Monica Boehme, Pastor Edward Eissabake, Suzanne and Daphne Eissabake

A smiling Louise Tamey holding a 1928 photo of the church

Louise Tamey hugging Milton David after 1928 photo presentation

Milton David examining church artifacts with Pastor Eissabake

Stained glass window of Christ praying in Gethsemane Garden

Large reception audience in the Social Hall

Elisha and Victoria David
Biography of Elisha David Contributed by Milton C. David, M.D.

Elisha David, oldest of four children, was born on 04 January 1881, in the village of "Seiri" about (about 5.6 miles) south of the city of Urmia, capital of Azerbaijan District. This village was located in the mountainous region between Lake Urmia and the Zagros mountains to the west. The claim to fame of Seiri was a natural spring (Eyena in Assyrian) still abundantly flowing today.

Elisha'a father David Lazar apparently suffered from alcoholism and went to Russia for long periods of time seeking work to support his family. As a result, Elisha's mother took on the task of raising the children in Seiri, by no means an easy task in those days.

The American Presbyterian Medical Mission was established in the city of Urmia in 1833. They provided medical help to the residents of Urmia, and other villages, including Seiri. It is at this time, that Elisha met Dr. Shedd and Dr. Cochran who were sponsored by the Fourth Presbyterian Church in Chicago. Dr. John Timothy

Stone was the senior pastor at 4th Presbyterian Church in Chicago. It was this exposure to doctors in the Christian faith that encouraged Elisha to go to America and study to be a Presbyterian minister. As a result, Dr. Stone sponsored Elisha David to study at the Dubuque Seminary of the University of Dubuque, in Iowa.

Elisha David came to America at the age 24 in 1905 along with some 25 other Assyrian young men. Their travels took them first to Russia and then onto England where they boarded a ship bound for New York. They were processed through the Immigration Center at Ellis Island. It is not clear how Elisha initially settled in upstate New York. Milton, his son, relates his father admitting that they froze in the very cold winters. He decided to move to the more friendly confines of Chicago, where he knew Dr. Stone. Elisha lived with Dr. Stone's family until he was admitted to Seminary. It was Dr. Stone's wish that Elisha remain in Chicago after graduation from Dubuque Seminary in 1923. He was now 42 years old.

It was quite common for Assyrians from Iran to come to America for work, save their money and send it to their families in the villages in the Lake Urmia area. In many instances, they would ask their parents to pick a bride and send her to America.

Elisha's next move after seminary was affected by a request from his first cousin Geroosha Addy. She asked him to come to Turlock and serve the Assyrian community and start a new Assyrian Presbyterian Church. She justified her request to cousin Elisha by stating that her request was based on the fact that there were about 150 Assyrian families living in the Turlock area and all had migrated from Urmia, Iran.

Dwight, Eleanor and Milton's mother, Victoria Esther Adams was born on 25 September 1905 in North Battleford, Saskatchewan, Canada. Their uncle, Dr. Isaac Adams and his wife Sarah were the first Assyrian family to come to Turlock in 1910. Rev. Dr. Isaac Adams had a nephew, Joseph Adams who was also a minister. The Isaac Adam's family was anxious to begin a Presbyterian church in Turlock. The early Assyrian settlers in Turlock could not afford to build a new church. As a result, the Adams family and a committee of Assyrians wrote a letter to Dr. Stone in Chicago indicating how poor they were, but rich in faith and requested that Rev. Elisha David be sent to Turlock. Rev. David arrived in Turlock in 1923 to evaluate his future with the un-churched Assyrians. He reiterated to the Assyrians in Turlock about his promise he made to Dubuque University whereby he would work for one year after graduation from seminary to help raise funds for needy foreign students. This experience put him in touch with several donors in the Chicago area for fund raising and opened hearts for needed gifts for the new church in Turlock.

Rev. Elisha returned to Turlock in 1925. Under the guidance of the Presbytery of San Joaquin, the first Assyrian Presbyterian Church in Turlock was established, serving Turlock and the San Francisco communities. Under the guidance of Rev. Elisha David, a committee was formed to select an architect. They traveled to Oakland to interview Rollin S. Tuttle. He was selected to design the new church. The church can be classified as Spanish in style. The contractor chosen was Thomas A. Cuthbertson from San Francisco. The majority of the construction labor was provided by volunteers from the Assyrian Community in Turlock. The church cost $21,000 and was dedicated by the Rev. Walter E. Edmunds on 16 December 1928. Dr. Stone came to visit the church from Chicago in 1932 and was amazed at what he saw.

During the first 30 years of its existence, the church was totally supported by the Board of National Missions. This organization was under the guidance of Dr. Phillip Payne, Director of the National Missions of the Presbyterian Church. Until the church became self-sufficient, only then were they able to pay Pastor David's salary. What with the Great Depression in 1929, America's ability to collect funds from taxpayers was greatly diminished. This was one of the main causes as to why the church could not become self-sufficient soon enough. Pastor David's family lived in a rental house near the church on East Avenue until the Manse was constructed in 1936.

Victoria Esther Adams David
Biography of Victoria David contributed by Eleanor David Huskins

Born 25 September 1905, North Battleford, Saskatchewan, Canada
Married Rev. Dr. Elisha David on 14 June 1926, Turlock, CA
Died 11 November 1996, Modesto, CA

Children: Dwight, Elisha, born 26 September 1929, Turlock, CA
Died 15 January 2002, Modesto, CA
Eleanor, Jean, born 31 July 1932, Turlock, CA
Milton Curtis born 21 May 1934, Turlock, CA

Education: Victoria was in the first graduating class of Turlock H.S. in 1924

Settling in Canada

Prior to immigrating to Canada, there were five Assyrian families living in Iran who discovered that Queen Victoria of Great Britain was offering tracts of land to increase the number of immigrants to populate this vast and sparse country. The Assyrian families that took advantage of this offer were the Adams, Balisha, Khoobyar, Backus and Lazar. Eventually, they all immigrated to America and settled in the Turlock/Livingston area.

Activities

Victoria participated in Women's Christian Temperance Society (WCTU). She was the first President of this Society. She organized and conducted the activities of Pre-school at the church. She supported her husband in teaching Sunday school and was deeply involved in the Women's Christian Association. She enjoyed participating in the annual 4th of July Parades in downtown Turlock. She taught the Assyrian language in church. She empowered personal independence for the church women and taught them how to drive cars.

She raised three children while participating in church related activities. As a homemaker, she loved to bake. She won a number of prizes for baking "Upside down Pineapple Cake" in the Stanislaus County Fair in Turlock.

To make life easier for her husband, she was a big supporter of him.

Pastor Biography
St. John's Assyrian Presbyterian Church
Turlock, California

Reverend Dr. Elisha David

1925 - 1954

Elisha and Victoria David

Elisha's biography contributed by Milton C. David, M.D.

Elisha David, oldest of four children, was born on 04 January1881, in the village of "Seiri" about (about 5.6 miles) south of the city of Urmia, capital of Azerbaijan District. This village was located in the mountainous region between Lake Urmia and the Zagros mountains to the west. The claim to fame of Seiri was a natural spring (Eyena in Assyrian) still abundantly flowing today.

Elisha'a father David Lazar apparently suffered from alcoholism and went to Russia for long periods of time seeking work to support his family. As a result, Elisha's mother took on the task of raising the children in Seiri, by no means an easy task in those days.

The American Presbyterian Medical Mission was established in the city of Urmia in 1833. They provided medical help to the residents of Urmia, and other villages, including Seiri. It is at this time, that Elisha met Dr. Shedd and Dr. Cochran who were sponsored by the Fourth Presbyterian Church in Chicago. Dr. John Timothy Stone was the senior pastor 4th Presbyterian Church in Chicago. It was this exposure to doctors in the Christian faith that encouraged Elisha to go to America and study to be a Presbyterian minister. As a result, Dr. Stone sponsored Elisha David to study at the Dubuque Seminary of the University of Dubuque, in Iowa.

Elisha David came to America at the age 24 in 1905 along with some 25 other Assyrian young men. Their travels took them first to Russia and then onto England where they boarded a ship bound for New York. They were processed through the Immigration Center at Ellis Island. It is not clear how Elisha initially settled in upstate New York. Milton, his son, relates his father admitting that they froze in the very cold winters. He decided to move to the more friendly confines of Chicago, where he knew Dr. Stone. Elisha lived with Dr. Stone's family until he was admitted to Seminary. It was Dr. Stone's wish that Elisha remain in Chicago after graduation from Dubuque Seminary in 1923. He was now 42 years old.

It was quite common for Assyrians from Iran to come to America for work, save their money and send it to their families in the villages in the Lake Urmia area. In many instances, they would ask their parents to pick a bride and send her to America.

Elisha's next move after seminary was affected by a request from his first cousin Geroosha Addy. She asked him to come to Turlock and serve the Assyrian community and start a new Assyrian Presbyterian Church. She justified her request to cousin Elisha by stating that her request was based on the fact that there were about 150 Assyrian families living in the Turlock area and all had migrated from Urmia, Iran.

Dwight, Eleanor and Milton's mother, Victoria Esther Adams was born on 25 September 1905 in North Battleford, Saskatchewan, Canada. Their uncle, Dr. Isaac Adams and his wife Sarah were the first Assyrian family to come to Turlock in 1910. Rev. Dr. Isaac Adams had a nephew, Joseph Adams who was also a minister. The Isaac Adam's family was anxious to begin a Presbyterian church in Turlock. The early Assyrian settlers in Turlock could not afford to build a new church. As a result, the Adams family and a committee of Assyrians wrote a letter to Dr. Stone in Chicago indicating how poor they were, but rich in faith and requested that Rev. Elisha David be sent to Turlock. Rev. David arrived in Turlock in 1923 to evaluate his future with the un-churched Assyrians. He reiterated to the Assyrians in Turlock about his promise he made to Dubuque University whereby he would work for one year after graduation from seminary to help raise funds for needy foreign students. This experience put him in touch with several donors in the Chicago area for fund raising and opened hearts for needed gifts for the new church in Turlock.

Rev. Elisha returned to Turlock in 1925. Under the guidance of the Presbytery of San Joaquin, the first Assyrian Presbyterian Church in Turlock was established, serving Turlock and the San Francisco communities. Under the guidance of Rev. Elisha David, a committee was formed to select an architect. They traveled to Oakland to interview Rollin S. Tuttle. He was selected to design the new church. The church can be classified as Spanish in style. The contractor chosen was Thomas A. Cuthbertson from San Francisco. The majority of the construction labor was provided by volunteers from the Assyrian Community in Turlock. The church cost $21,000 and was dedicated by the Rev. Walter E. Edmunds on 16 December 1928. Dr. Stone came to visit the church from Chicago in 1932 and was amazed at what he saw.

During the first 30 years of its existence, the church was totally supported by the Board of National Missions. This organization was under the guidance of Dr. Phillip Payne, Director of the National Missions of the Presbyterian Church. Until the church became self-sufficient, only then were they able to pay Pastor David's salary. What with the Great Depression in 1929, America's ability to collect funds from taxpayers was greatly diminished. This was one of the main causes as to why the church could not become self-sufficient soon enough. Pastor David's family lived in a rental house near the church on East Avenue until the Manse was constructed in 1936.

Victoria Esther Adams David
Biography contributed by Eleanor David Huskins

Born 25 September 1905, North Battleford, Saskatchewan, Canada

Married Rev. Dr. Elisha David on 14 June 1926, Turlock, CA

Died 11 November 1996, Modesto, CA

Children: Dwight, Elisha, born 26 September 1929, Turlock, CA

Died 15 January 2002, Modesto, CA

Eleanor, Jean, born 31 July 1932, Turlock, CA

Milton Curtis born 21 May 1934, Turlock, CA

Education: Victoria was in the first graduating class of Turlock H.S. in 1924

Settling in Canada

Prior to immigrating to Canada, there were five Assyrian families living in Iran who discovered that Queen Victoria of Great Britain was offering tracts of land to increase the number of immigrants to populate this vast and sparse country. The Assyrian families that took advantage of this offer were the Adams, Balisha, Khoobyar, Backus and Lazar. Eventually, they all immigrated to America and settled in the Turlock/Livingston area.

Activities

Victoria participated in Women's Christian Temperance Society (WCTU). She was the first President of this Society. She organized and conducted the activities of Pre-school at the church. She supported her husband in teaching Sunday school and was deeply involved in the Women's Christian Association. She enjoyed participating in the annual 4th of July Parades in downtown Turlock. She taught the Assyrian language in church. She empowered personal independence for the church women and taught them how to drive cars.

She raised three children while participating in church related activities. As a homemaker, she loved to bake. She won a number of prizes for baking "Upside down Pineapple Cake" in the Stanislaus County Fair in Turlock.

To make life easier for her husband, she was a big supporter of him.

Dubuque University Theological Seminary 1923
Elisha David, middle row, second from right

Victoria and Elisha David
1905-1996   1881-1976

1926 Church met during construction in the basement.
Rev. Elisha David is on the right, seated fourth, front row

Dedication of the church
December 16, 1928

1940 Family picture
Victoria and Rev. Elisha David, Eleanor, Dwight and Milton

Pastor Biography
St. John's Assyrian Presbyterian Church
Turlock, California

Reverend Stephen O. Khoobyar

1956 - 1961

Rev. Stephen Odishoo Khoobyar
Biography contributed by Milt Khoobyarian

Pastor Stephen Khoobyar was born on 20 April 1895 as the second child of Odishoo and Ensap Khoobyar. Stephen grew up in the village of Ada attending the Presbyterian Mission for elementary and high school then to college at the Presbyterian College in Urmia. In addition to mastering his native Assyrian language, he learned Turkish, Farsi, and English. The College in Urmia also offered a degree in Theology that Stephen pursued and completed.

Hamaspure, future wife of Stephen, nicknamed (Piour), was born on 10 May 1898. Piour, attended the same elementary and secondary schools as Stephen, in Ada. Thus Stephen and Piour grew up in the same close environment although it is unknown if they ever shared a class. When Piour was asked how Stephen and she courted, she replied "Oh, there was never any formal courting involved. It was understood that when the parents of a couple approved, then their marriage could take place." According to the family Bible, Stephen and Piour were married on 24 May 1916 in Ada. The ceremony was held in the Presbyterian Church of Ada and was officiated by the Rev. Shmuel Americas. While in school, Stephen was hired by the Mission to assist with the Evangelistic work of the Presbyterian Church. This consisted of teaching and preaching the Gospel in Assyrian as well as Turkish language(s) among all inhabitants. Eventually Stephen completed his studies in Theology.

(The Great War (WW1) broke out in Europe in June 1914. By winter of 1914 two of the main protagonists, the Ottoman Empire (currently Turkey and Iraq) and the Czarist Empire (currently Russia) had their armies poised for battle on two borders of Azerbaijan, Iran.

In October 1914, the District of Urmia, was invaded by Turkish troops and Kurdish irregulars. For a time they were successful in resisting the counterattack of the Russians and in plundering and destroying the (Assyrian) villages until a new contingency of Russian reinforcements were brought in to save the city. By the end of December, 1914 the Russian army was defeated at the border and news was spread by the Rev. Dr. William A. Shedd, head of the Presbyterian Church Mission of Urmia and the surrounding townships, that the Russian army was planning to withdraw all its troops. People were advised to leave their homes and if possible flee with the Russian troops as they headed north. On Jan. 2, 1915 the entire Russian army withdrew from Urmia. This was the emergency signal to all Christian inhabitants to leave for safety because the local Persian government was unprepared or unwilling to control the situation once the Turkish army entered the country. Kurdish irregulars preceding the Turkish army started the looting of all Assyrian villages, taking everything, threatening and killing those who resisted their plundering. A mass exodus of those in proximity of the Russian army made the dash to the Russian border. The remaining panic-stricken refugees raced towards the foreign Mission compounds in the city of Urmia. Three thousand were taken by the French Catholic Mission and seventeen thousand found refuge in the American Presbyterian Mission. Many unfortunate ones could not escape the onslaught and were overtaken and perished. Per Dr. Shedd's observation, two thousand people died on the first day alone as they tried to reach the Presbyterian Mission sanctuary. Other Assyrians fled south and eventually reached the city of Hamadan, 400 miles away where there was a garrison British Troops to protect them.

On April 21, 1917 Stephen and Piour had their first child, a boy they named Hayrik born in Ada. Unfortunately, due to lack of proper medical care, Hayrick's short life ended on Jan. 25, 1918.

In Hamadan camps were set up by the British army to process and settle the refugees as they scattered in. Refugees consisted of many groups and backgrounds. The bulk of the population was Urmia Assyrians. Recall that in Iran there were also large populations of Armenians who were also being displaced in Azerbaijan as well as a large group of mountain Assyrians from Iraq who were chased from their villages in northern Iraq by the Turkish army and assisted by their Kurdish vassals. For this group the British army built additional camps in Baquba, Mesopotamia (modern Iraq). The British Officer in charge of settlements in Hamadan camp was Capt. George F. Gracey. Per Piour, Stephen was hired by Capt. Gracey to serve as his translator.

On October 18, 1918, Stephen and Piour had their second child, a daughter they named Helen born in Hamadan. Piour recalled that the British military office in Hamadan wanted to keep Stephen employed for a longer duration. However, as soon as the political conditions settled in Azerbaijan people began to return to their homes in Urmia. Stephen and Piour decided to do the same since they had their remaining aging relatives with which to concern themselves. In Urmia the returning refugees were required to register with the authorities and obtain a document that was called

'Sejeel' as proof of birth and citizenship. Piour recalls that Stephen's father Odishoo went to the police station and filed all the required paperwork for the entire family. It was at this time that the family surname was appended by adding the suffix of 'ian' to Khoobyar. The "ian" was dropped several years later when Stephen and Piour became United States citizens. However, their sons Newton and Milton kept the "ian" due to difficulty of having incompatible records.

By the end of 1921 British and Russian troops had left Iran and life in Azerbaijan began to slowly return to peacetime. Stephen began his next assignment from the Presbyterian Church Mission to become the pastor of the Tabriz Evangelical Presbyterian Church. Thus in 1921, Stephen, Piour and Helen moved to Tabriz, the largest city in Azerbaijan Province and its capitol. On Dec. 14, 1921 Stephen and Piour had another child, a boy they named Nathan born in Tabriz.

During all the years of his ministry in various churches and his associations with people of all religions who came to know Stephen, considered him a true friend and an inspiring preacher. His passion for preaching the Christian message and his understanding and expressing the power of the Christian faith were hallmark of his ministry.

Stephen's talents brought him to the attention of the American Mission and they offered him a one-year scholarship to do post graduate work at Princeton Theological Seminary, Princeton, NJ (1924 -1925). While Stephen was in Princeton, on Oct. 20, 1924 Stephen and Piour had another child, a boy they named Newton born in Tabriz.

In 1925, Reza Khan Pahlavi, a former cavalry officer in the Persian army, eventually took over the monarchy by ousting Ahmad Shah the last king of the Qajar dynasty. It was during Reza Shah Pahlavi's direction that a decree was passed to replace the name of the country from 'Persia' to 'Iran'.

During the period 1930 - 1940 Stephen and Piour faced several challenges: family sicknesses, travels that separated them, preparations for Church Centennial celebrations, and a growing church. On Oct. 16, 1930 Nathan came down with a sickness that was not diagnosed resulting in his passing at the age of 8 years and 10 months.

WW II brought disruptions to the life of the Khoobyar family. As a result of Lend-

Lease between USSR and America, Russian troops were stationed in Azerbaijan Province to protect the armaments sent by America via roads from the Persian Gulf to Russia. Similarly, British troops in the southern part of Iran provided for protection of armaments shipped by truck to Russia from the Persian Gulf. These war activities disrupted the normal life of the Khoobyar family. Life slowly became more difficult during the occupation. Its effect on the economy began to show everywhere. Milton recalls, 'The bakery next door making bread every morning for the occupiers.' Every morning a Russian army truck would come to pick up a full load of bread. At times the regular customers were not able to buy their bread while this was in process and had to return later. This type of activity must have gone on throughout the city, which began to fulfill the demands of thousands of unplanned foreign troops.

Family Separated

During the early 1940s secondary schools in Tabriz were maxed through twelfth grade since there was no university level graduate program. For the fall semester of 1942-1943, Helen went to Tehran to attend graduate studies at the Sage College under the Presbyterian Mission. Upon completion of her studies, she was offered a teaching position at the Community School (high school level) in Tehran. This school provided enrollment for non-Iranian students in a co-educational setting. Hence the student body consisted mostly of missionary, diplomatic, and other foreign dependents.

Similarly, in 1943 Newton followed Helen to Tehran to purse his university studies at the Alborz College. With both Helen and Newton moving to Tehran it was necessary to rent an apartment there where Piour and Milton later joined them. Milton enrolled at the Mehr Elementary School, also run by the Presbyterian Mission of Tehran.

The family being split was financially very difficult for Stephen and Piour. The cost of rent, food, and gas for heating in Tehran was extremely high. War years had affected Iran's economy with shortages in all areas resulting in exorbitant inflation rates that reduced the purchasing power of families living in Tehran. Stephen referred to a price increase of up to 80% in Tabriz during the period 1943 - 1945. For a long time there were no price controls in place. Much later when rents skyrocketed, the government in Tehran imposed controls in that city. In Tehran the family's apartment rent went up several times and someone had told Newton what paperwork was needed to plea for reduction. Newton and Milton went to the office of government that handled complaints and Newton filled out the request. Fortunately Stephen's sister Sophia and her husband Yacoub were still in Tabriz living next door to Stephen, which helped by sharing some of the expenses of both households.

Start of family migration to America

Before the completion of the academic year in 1946, Helen and Newton had applied to colleges in the U.S. with student visas. Each was accepted at a Presbyterian affiliated college, Helen at the College of Wooster in Wooster, Ohio and Newton at Lafayette College in Easton, PA. They started their long journey from Iran by air to India and from India on a refurbished navy ship to San Francisco, CA. This was the biggest separation in the family and one that kept the family wondering what would be coming next. Of course, at that time none of us realized that this was indeed the last time the family would be together.

Stephen and Piour continued their ministry in Tabriz until Stephen was called to serve as a pastor of the South Congregational Church's Assyrian Mission in New Britain, CT. On July 2, 1948 Stephen, Piour and Milton arrived in New York and were greeted by Helen and Newton who had preceded them to America by two years. At the South Church, Stephen preached regularly to both the English and Assyrian speaking congregations. Piour immediately enrolled in an adult education course that taught English and preparation for prospective citizens. Milton was interviewed by the Principal of the New Britain Senior High School. He was assigned to the tenth grade academic curriculum. Since Milton's plans were to continue his education to college he was told to also include a foreign language (French or German) in his curriculum since none of the four languages that he already knew (Armenian, Assyrian, Turkish, and Farsi) would qualify as college entrance requirement. Learning a new language was never one of Milton's favorite pastimes he obviously was disappointed. He selected French.

After graduating from New Britain Senior High School in June 1951 Milton attended the College of Wooster in Wooster, Ohio graduating in June of 1955 with a major in Applied Mathematics. Helen continued her graduate studies at Northwestern University, Evanston, IL, (MA English), Hartford Seminary Foundation, Hartford, CT, (BD and MA Religious Education), University of

California at Berkeley, (PhD Philosophy). Helen's career path was Director of Religious Education in various churches and teaching at the Hartford Seminary Foundation, and in Sacramento teaching philosophy at various junior colleges. Newton continued his graduate studies at the University of Illinois, Urbana, (MS Microbiology), University of Wisconsin, (PhD Microbiology). Career path included microbiologist at the University of Indiana and the University of Illinois. Milton's career began in Mannheim, West Germany with the U.S. Army via Selective Service Administration, 1955-1957. He then taught high school math at San Lorenzo Valley, CA, State of California, Department of Water Resources, Sacramento CA, management of Application Programming for eight years, IBM Corporation, San Jose, CA, management of Systems Analysts and Programmers for 31 years.

In 1956 Stephen accepted a call from the San Joaquin Presbytery in CA to become pastor of the St. John's Assyrian Presbyterian Church of Turlock, CA. He served there until his retirement in 1961 and died on January 11, 1962. Piour decided to relocate to Sacramento, CA where Helen and Milton also resided. Piour became active in Fremont Presbyterian Church in Sacramento until her death on May 11, 1989.

During his early ministry in Urmia, Stephen authored several pamphlets in Assyrian and translated some from English to Assyrian, which were printed by the Presbyterian Mission's press in Urmia. One article in English titled 'The privilege of Preaching to Moslems" illustrates his passion for the lifelong challenge he embraced in evangelizing among the Mohammedans.

Stephen's sermons, pastoral prayers, speeches, and papers in both English and Assyrian languages that he preached since arriving in the U.S. were all kept in handwritten folders neatly preserved. These were organized and converted into digital form as a document which is also accessible on the web:

http://sites.google.com/site/sermonsbykhoobyar

Khoobyar Family 1961
Newton, Helen, Milton, Piour, Stephen

Reverend Dr. Stephen Odishoo Khoobyar 1958

Hamaspure (Piour) Khoobyar 1958

Pastor Biography
St. John's Assyrian Presbyterian Church
Turlock, California

Reverend Darius Baba Yohannan

1963 - 1983

Reverend Darius Baba Yohannan
Biography contributed by Nancy S. Yohannan

Darius Baba Yohannan was born to Baba and Selby Yohannan on 30 December 1907 in the village of Digaleh, located in Urmia District of Iran. He passed away on 14 September 1987 in Turlock, CA.

Devotion to his father, mother and others:

Uprooted by the Assyrian and Armenian Genocide of 1914, Christians were compelled to escape from their villages to the safety of the British-occupied neighboring country of Iraq. It was during this time that all of Darius' extended family immigrated to America save for Darius and his parents. Once it was safe to return to Urmia, Darius' father, Baba, went to unearth the family bible he had hidden for safekeeping during the genocide and found it to be missing. Baba had been tasked with caring for it by the dying wish of his brother (who himself was a pastor) who was hanged during the genocide. This bible was 800 years old at the time, as old as the eight generations of priests going back in Darius' family tree. Thinking it was lost forever, Darius' father grew so ill with guilt that Darius had to carry his father piggyback from Urmia to the village of Digaleh on foot, a distance of some 3 miles. Although dying shortly after returning home, this act of love and devotion to his dying father serves as the greatest metaphor for Darius' entire life, selfless and willing to carry burdens that others could or would not.

He joined the American Presbyterian Seminary in Urmi at the urging of his mother where he received his degree in Theology in June of 1933. In the years that followed he completed a tour of service with the Iranian Army from 1934-1938. Shortly after being discharged from the Iranian military, World War II broke out in 1939. Darius' conscience urged him to join the fight against Hitler. Darius enlisted in the British Army as a translator. Unknown to anyone else at the time he was also under secret orders tasked with espionage to help defeat the Nazi influences in the Middle Eastern regions. It was during this time that he became fluent in English, various dialects from India, and Hebrew. These were in addition to the Assyrian, Farsi, Turkish, and Arabic languages he had been assigned as translator. This meant that he spoke a total of seven languages by the year 1949 to help him spread his devotion of the word of God. Receiving news that his mother was dying while still in the army, Darius rushed back to the village from India. However, due to the vastly oversaturated methods of transportation in those early post-war years, he was not able to make it in time to pay his last respects to his mother.

Marriage to Lily Shlemon:

Darius eventually settled back into his life at the village of Digaleh, asking for Lily Shlemon's hand in marriage and was wed on 31 December 1947. Lily was born in Baghdad, Iraq on Christmas Day, 25 December 1921. Shortly after his marriage Darius was honorably discharged as a decorated sergeant in the British Army in the fall of 1949.

It was in writing to his family in America to announce his marriage that Darius received word that the bible his father presumed lost forever, had been taken from its hiding place in Iraq to America and had been sold to an unknown individual who had donated it to the Smithsonian Institute in Washington, D.C.

From 1949 until 1955 in addition to helping to nurture the family vineyards, Darius also served as Principal Dean for the Assyrian schools throughout the District of Urmia as well as working as a church layman during his travels.

Darius and Lily start their family:

Darius and Lilly had three children, Nancy, Jaleh and Jordan by the year 1954. It was at this point that Darius was ordained to be the pastor of the Urmi's (then known as Rezaieh) Presbyterian church announced his departure. The local elders brought in every ordained minister in the area for the village to vote for. Politics, however, resulting in the church's doors being closed. The Presbyterian mission was notified and since Darius had attended their seminary he was asked via written letter to keep the church's doors open until they could address the situation. Darius ministered to the people of Urmi's church every Sunday until the representatives from the Presbyterian mission finally arrived. It was at this point that Darius was ordained to be the pastor of the Urmi's church. Darius always said that he had never intended to be the pastor for Urmia's Presbyterian congregation but he could not help but feel that God's hand was involved and was soon thereafter ordained by the Presbyterian Mission in 1956.

First assignment as Pastor of the church of Urmia:

His congregation steadily increased as those from the villages heard his sermons and all members were anxious to do more for the church. Darius led a bible study every Friday for children and young adults from all denominations. He also organized afternoon classes to be held every day after school for the children to learn to read and write Assyrian. He also taught bible study to converted Iranians in the privacy of his home. There were many other programs set up such as women's auxiliaries where clothes, aprons, dresses, etc. were made for the needy Assyrians in the nearby cities and the villages. As every pastor used to do in the old days, he took the time to visit parishioners far and wide, sick and healthy, throughout the entire region of Urmia.

Something he was most proud of was being able to help the people of all the surrounding villages within the District of Urmia. They would come to him with nothing and because of Darius' standing within the church he was able to send with them letters that would provide for free medical treatment. He would arrange for the transport of, or sometimes transport them himself, to the mission hospital in Tabriz which was the only nearby place with advanced medical care.

Darius' Faith in God and education:

Darius accomplished so much in Iran through faith alone. In 1961 the roof of the church, which had been built in the late 19th century, was destroyed through age and weather. Although there weren't sufficient funds to replace the roof Darius decided to go ahead and begin the renovations regardless of finances. Darius promised that God would provide and He did, so much so that not only was the roof replaced, but the church received chandeliers for the church's nave. He also arranged for the erection of the bell tower. One of the final things he accomplished before his departure was requisitioning the former American military base of Rezaieh through his friendship with the American officers, and transforming it into a non-denominational hostel for the students who lived in villages too remote to attend school because Darius was a great believer in education.

Throughout this time in his life he was Chairman of the Board of Education for all American Mission Schools in Northwestern Iran and the Presbyterian Board of the Foreign Mission from 1954-1963. He was also the Overseer of all churches in Rezaieh (present day Urmia) from 1954-1956 a position from which he stepped down when he was ordained as the minister of the Church of Urmi from 1956-1963.

Pastor of St. John's Assyrian Presbyterian Church, Turlock, CA

In March 1963, Reverend Darius B. Yohannan was called by the congregation of St. John's Presbyterian Church in Turlock, California, United States, to come from Iran to be their pastor. After leaving the Presbyterian Church of Urmi in the hands of his old friend and colleague from Seminary, Reverend Sargis Sayad, Darius and his family immigrated to the United States in 1963.

His first sermon at St. John's Assyrian Presbyterian Church in Turlock, California was on Easter Day, 14 April 1963. For the next 20 years Darius served as a beloved pastor and father figure to countless Assyrians both newly arrived and long settled. During these years he was invited to be a speaker and have the honor as a moderator at the Presbytery in Philadelphia, which was the first Presbytery ever built in 1706. In addition he and two elders would attend the monthly Presbytery meetings in Stockton, CA. to represent the Assyrian-Presbyterian congregations of the surrounding areas.

Just as in Iran, when the missionaries would stay at his house for months at a time, so too did the Assyrians in Turlock who had come to this country destitute. Darius and Lily always welcomed these strangers and treated them as family. The same man who visited the sick in Iran visited the sick in Turlock at the hospitals and prayed with men and women of all ethnic origins and denominations. The nurses and doctors at Emmanuel Hospital in Turlock would be the only voice of the unconscious or the dying who had no friends or family with them and asked Darius to pray for them which he would always do. Visiting the nearby prison and praying with inmates was something he looked forward to doing as well.

Reverend Yohannan never forgot the church in Urmi, returning in 1969 to visit, and often keeping up with correspondence with Reverend Sargis and the Elders. When his son returned to visit Iran with his wife and child, also named Darius, they were surrounded by his parishioners and other Assyrians whom he had never met his children. They eagerly shared common stories of his kindness towards them.

In 1983 he retired, returning to caring for the land and cultivating it as he had done in his youth back in Iran. After his retirement on June 01, 1983, he was given the title, Pastor Emeritus by the Stockton Presbytery. His wife, Lily B. Yohannan, continued to help with the church auxiliary, always there to provide a helping hand with cooking and preparing meals for the congregation, their picnics, and memorials.

On Monday, September 14, 1987 Darius passed away and on Saturday, September 19th was put to rest in Turlock. On Good Friday, 2 April 2010, his wife Lily B. Yohannan passed in San Jose, CA. The Reverend Darius B. Yohannan lived his life to the end as it had begun, humble and pious. They are survived by their three children, Nancy, Jordan & Jaleh, as well as Jordan's wife, Janet, Jaleh's husband, George, along with their three grandchildren, Demator, Babalonia, and Darius.

Wedding of Darius and Lily Yohannan
Baghdad, Iraq, 1947

Pastor Darius preparing for Easter communion 1982
St. John's Assyrian Presbyterian Church

Church members posing for a group picture 1979
Pastor Darius Yohannan with Lincoln Abraham in front
Mike Benjamin Sr. to left of Lincoln Abraham
Lily Yohannan second person down from end of stair railing

November 1978

Top row: Eva Marr, Lily Eshoo, Rev. Darius Yohannan, Babajan Assur **Second row:** Maria Rustam, Sargis Givargis, **Third row:** Margaret Quishahpur, Bulbul Baddell, Katia Avroo, unknown, **Fourth row:** Frieda Bilou, Nesta George, Maria Ameer, unkown, **Fifth row:**

Lily, Jalet and Pastor Darius in church grounds 1962

Pastor Biography
St. John's Assyrian Presbyterian Church
Turlock, California

Rev. Dr. George Shahbaz
1983 - 2003

Biography: Rev. Dr. George Shahbaz

Contributed through interview in July, 2017

Pastor George Shahbaz was born on 25 May 1944 and raised in the village of Anhar, Urmia, Iran.

His father, Nestorius (George) Shahbaz Sr., was born in 1909 in the village of Anhar, about seven (7) miles northwest of the city of Urmia. His mother, Beatrice Badalian was born on 15 May 1915 in the village of Diza about two (2) miles from Urmia. Nestorius and Beatrice were married in 1937 in the village of Anhar.

The Senior Shahbaz family raised four children; Florence, Marlene, George and John. All the siblings live in America.

Biography: Amal Nashif

Amal Nashif was born on 23 December 1944 in Beirut, Lebanon to an American-born mother, Salwa Nashif and Lebanese father Elias Nashif. Amal married George Shahbaz on 26 September 1970 in Beirut.

Children:

Philip Shahbaz, was born on 01 July 1974 in Chicago, IL. He married Amy Chessum on 15 July 2000 in Los Angeles, CA. They have been blessed with quadruplet children; three sons, Jeremiah, Jordan, Jonah and daughter, Cedar, born on 28 March 2007 in Los Angeles.

Philip Shahbaz, serves as one of seven (7) Pastors at the Life Bible Fellowship Church in Upland, CA.

Peter Shahbaz, was born on 19 November 1983 in Turlock, CA. He is single and lives in the Los Angeles area.

Education: Pastor George Shahbaz:

George attended grade school in Kirkuk, and high school in Baghdad, Iraq.

After high school, George attended Ankara University, Turkey, from 1966 to 1968 and received a diploma in the Turkish language.

A tutor was retained at Anhar village to teach George the English language. George was introduced to the Southern Baptist faith by American Missionary Jim Leeper, while still in Turkey.

From 1968 to 1971 The Galatian Baptist Mission sponsored George to the Baptist Theological Seminary, Beirut Lebanon. He acquired a B.A. degree in Theology.

George and Amal, emigrated from Lebanon to America in 1971 and made their home in Chicago, IL.

Prior to being ordained, on 25 February 1973, George served in all phases of ministry and specifically with the youth in Chicago. Rev. Shahbaz served in the capacity of pastor/missionary for the Assyrian Baptist Ministry while at Lake Shore Baptist Church in Chicago, IL.

In 1974, George acquired a Masters degree in Arts and Religion and a Master of Divinity from the American Baptist Theological Seminary of the West, in Berkeley, CA.

In 1975, pastor George received a Doctor of Philosophy degree in Counseling Psychology from Carolina University of Theology in North Carolina.

In 1983, Pastor George Shahbaz was appointed by the Stockton Presbytery to serve as pastor of St. John's Assyrian Presbyterian Church in Turlock, CA. For the next 20 years, working with the Session, he fulfilled his role as pastor by preaching, providing guidance in Sunday school, bible study, youth groups, men's groups and women's associations. In addition, he preached the Word on radio and television in Stanislaus County. He worked to assist Christian refugees from Iran and Iraq through the auspices of the Stockton Presbytery.

In 2015 Rev. Shahbaz was appointed pastor of the United Assyrian Evangelical Church, Turlock, CA

Amal's church activities 1983- 2003

Active in Women's Christian Organization and assisted in Pre-school. She supported her husband in church and in Sunday school activities.

She raised two children while still serving St. John's Assyrian Presbyterian Church. In addition to being a homemaker, she loved to bake.

1970 wedding Picture in Beirut, Lebanon
Elias Nashif, George & Amal Shahbaz, Salwa Nashif

Family picture in Upland, CA
Philip, Amy, Jonah, Pastor George, Jeremiah, Amal,
Cedar, Cousin Remah, Peter

2009, Grandpa George with Jordan
Cedar, Jeremiah and Jonah

Pastor Biography
St. John's Assyrian Evangelical Presbyterian Church
Turlock, California

Reverend Edward William Eissabake

2003 - Present

Rev. Edward William Eissabake
Biogtaphy contributed by Rev. Eissabake

The Early Family years:

Rev. Edward William Eissabake was born as an Assyrian on 19 May, 1963 to the late Eprim (AKA: William) Eissabake and Maryam (AKA: Heyghanoosh) Stepanian in Hamadan, Iran. Edward's mother is half Armenian from her father's side. Edward was baptized as an infant in the Roman Catholic denomination. He was the youngest among his siblings (Joseph and Claudette). Currently, his brother lives in Germany and his sister lives in Tehran, Iran. He relocated from Hamadan along with his family to Tehran at the age of five. He attended elementary school and completed high school, studying Physcis and Mathematics at Kharazmi High School in Tehran.

At the age of 15 he attended St. Thomas Assyrian Evangelical Presbyterian Church of Tehran. He accepted Jesus Christ as his personal savior when he was 17 years old during a summer retreat sponsored by the Synod of the Evangelical Presbyterian Church of Iran held at Evangelism Garden, (in Farsi, Bagheh Beshart).

First exposure to the Evangelical Presbyterian Church:

Edward was called as a candidate to ministerial education by the Session of the St. Thomas Assyrian Evangelical Presbyterian Church of Iran in 1979. He graduated from the Divinity School of Evangelical Presbyterian Church of Iran under the supervision of the Board of Education of the Synod of Iran. In addition, he completed full courses of Campus Crusade for the Christ- Middle East Chapter in 1983.

He was a member of the Board of Education of the Synod of the Evangelical (Presbyterian) Church (ECI) of Iran for many years and one of the professors at the Divinty School of ECI.

With recommendations from two Assyrian Scholars: the late Robi Isa Benyamin and the late Robi Nimrod Simono and confirmation by the Assyrian Council of Tehran (Mottva), Edward taught the Assyrian language at the widely known Sossan Assyrian High School for two years. In preparation for teaching the Assyrian language, he was homeschooled by his late father Eprim. This effort was culminated by his Sunday School teacher, Miss Davis at St.Thomas Evangelical Presbyterian Chuch of Tehran.

His hunger for maturation of the Assyrian language continued by enhancing his exposure to other noted teachers.

He was an active member and the Secretary of the Presbytery of Iran for Assyrian churches for many years and he was introduced and recommended by the Presbytery of the Assyrian Evangelical Presbyterian of Iran as a candidate to be ordanied as a minister of Word and Sacrament in 1986. However, since he was single, he preferred to postpone his ordination and to be ordained as a married minister. He excused himself for the following reasons: 1) to establish his family life first and 2) to advance and continue his education to higher levels by studying in Lebanon, Netherlands and Switzerland. While employed by the St. Thomas Assyrian Evangelical Presbyterian Church of Tehran, he held different ministries such as: Assistant Pastor, Youth Director, Christian Educator, Evangelism Coordinator, etc.

He was employed by the Synod of the Evangelical Presbyterian Church of Iran as the Director of the Christian Ministries and Evangelism Coordinator from 1994-1996 prior to leaving Iran in 1996 to come to America.

Exposure to Iranian Military and publishing/translating newsletters:

Edward recognized the need to learn the English language so that he could report and transmit written information in both Farsi and English. To achieve this goal, he studied English under the proctorship of a British teacher at Kharazmi High School in Tehran. Part of the instruction involved listening to audio tapes to improve word pronunciation.

Edward joined the Iraninan Military as a Second Lieutenant and served his two-year mandatory service from 1991-1993. During these years, he wrote many articles to local Newspapers in Farsi and English, such as "Keyhan" and other well-known magazines in Tehran. In addition, he translated some articles and books from English to Farsi. He was the co-translator of "Halley's Bible Handbook" by Henry H. Halley from English to Farsi.

He Published monthly bulletins of the " Bright Morning Star" at St. Thomas Assyrian Evangelical Presbyterian Church of Tehran.

In addition, he published the monthly Magazine of "Ichthys," (Greek word for fish, symbol of Christianity) a spiritual and educational resource for ministers at the Synod of the Evangelical (Presbyterian) Church of Iran.

Interim Pastor, Marriage & call to serve as fulltime Pastor, Assyrian Evangelical Church of Turlock, CA:

Edward served as the Interim Pastor of the Persian Presbyterain Emanuel Church in Tehran for two years (1993-1995).

Pastor Edward married Suzanne Lazarof, daughter of George and Herosh Lazarof of Tehran on 24 March, 1995.

He received a call from Assyrian Evangelical Church of Turlock, CA in 1995 to be their future pastor of the church since their Pastor was retiring. To expedite this request, he traveled to Athens Greece in 02 January, 1996 in order to get a visa to travel to USA. His daughter Daphne Eissabake was born in Athens in 1996. He arrived in the USA on 25 September, 1996.

He was ordanied on 8 May, 1999 at the request of the Assyrian Evangelical Church of Turlock, Ca, and approval by the Synod of the Evangelical Presbyterian Church of Iran and the Middle Eastern Office of PCUSA and Global Ministries of PCUSA in Louisville, Kentucky.

He served the Assyrian Evangelical Church (AEC) of Turlock (a non-denominational church with a Presbyterian background) for 5 years until 2001 when his five-year contract was to terminate. After many prayers and reflection, Edward knew that God had something else in mind for him. Although the congregation unanimousley extended a call to him as their senior pastor. He did not renew his contract with the AEC of Turlock.

He continued his graduate theological education with the Trinity College and Seminary in Indiana and other Reformed Seminaries in Europe.

He was one of the co-founders of the Iranian Presbyterian Church and Fellowships in Northern America (ANJOMAN); established in 2000 in Washington D.C. He was elected as the Moderator of the Iranian Presbyterian Churches & Fellowships in Northern America from 2006-2007. In addition, he held several positions as the Vice-moderator and the Secretary of ANJOMAN.

He always believed in serving not only at a local congregation but to be involved in the community as well. He was employed by the Stanislaus Community Services Agency (CSA), and other local departments in 2001. In addition, Edward was employed by the Central Valley Foster Care, Inc. in April 2002 as the Social Work Supervisor. Currently he is with the same organization.

New addition to the family:

On 25 April, 2004, his son, Donton Eissabke was born in Modesto, California.

Associations with other church organizations:

Pastor Edward was involved with the New Church Development (NCD) and church planning of the PCUSA and also the Iranian Fellowships and served the Good Shephered Presbyterian Iranian church/fellowship in Seattle, WA. He also served as the Interim Pastor of Iranian Presbyterian Church (NCD-New Church Development), Seattle, WA. (2001-2003).

From 2001-2004 he was active in community activities and services outside of the church setting by holding different positions such as: Training Unity of the Modesto Police Department; Stanislaus County Department of Child Support Services (DCSS); Stanislaus County Community Services Agency (CSA) and the EE's 9, a Residential Group Home in San Jose, Ca.

Edward also served the Assyrian Evangelical church of San Jose, Ca. for three years as the interim pastor from 2002-2005. At the same time he was pastoring to the needs of St. John's Assyrian Presbyterian church in Turlock starting in 2003. The reason was that Assyrians had limited access to ordained ministers and needed time to make a "Call" on a potential minister to serve their church needs. It was God's calling that hastened Edward to serve two churches simultaeneosly.

Call from the Stockton Presbytery to serve as temporary Pastor at St. John's Assyrian Presbyterian Church:

Edward received a call from the Stockton Presbytery PC (USA) and Sirerra Mission Partnership to serve as the Temporary Supply for St. John's Assyrian Presbyterian Church of Turlock, CA in July of 2003 and took the ordination/installation examinations on August 25 and 26, 2006 at the San Francisco Theological Seminary, Ca. He was called and welcomed to be the full-time pastor of the St. John's since 2005. He was installed offically as the full-time pastor for St. John's by the Stockton Presbytery, PC (USA).

In addition, from 2011-2013 he was actively invloved in ecclesiastical ministeries such as: Stockton Presbytery commissioner to the Synod of Pacific- PC (USA) (2008-2012); Chairman of Committee on Representation (COR)-Synod of Pacific (PCUSA); Member of the Coordinating Council of Synod of Pacific (PCUSA)- 2008-2012; Vice Moderator and Moderator of the Synod of Pacific (PCUSA) from 2009-2011; Member of the Coordinating Council and Chairman of Committee on Representation (COR) of Stockton Presbytery (PCUSA) from 2009-2013; Member of the Education Committee of the Middle Eastern Caucus (PCUSA) from 2011-2013.

He finished his Doctoral Education with the Pastor as Spiritual Leader Concentration of Doctor of Ministry (D.Min) program at the San Francisco Theological Seminary (SFTS) in 2014.

An eye towards the community at large:

Pastor Edwrad was a co-founder and an active member of the Stanislaus County Assyrian Wellness Collaborative in partnership with Stanislaus County Mental Healh Deaprtment and was elected as the first Chairman of the Collaboration in 2014.

Pastor Edward was an active member and the Secretary of the Assyrian Interdenominational Council of Churches in Stanislaus County, Ca. He served as the Secretary of the council from 2006-2009.

Pastor Edward completed Clinical Pastoral Educaton (CPE) full courses of Chaplaincy in 2014 with the College of Pastoral and Supervision Psychotherapy (CPSP) of Transitioning Pathways LLC. He was an active member of Jacksonville Chapter of Chaplaincy in achieving his National Board Certification. This chapter is an "Online gathering." The members of this chapter are from the states of Colorado, California, New York and Massachusetts.

St. John's Assyrian Evangelical Presbyterian Church of Turlock joined Evangelcail Presbyterian Church (EPC) denomination in 2014 and Pastor Edward was examined and installed as the official minister of the Word and Sacrament by the Presbytery of Pacific of the Evangelcal Presbyterian Church (EPC) in 2014.

Exposure to Christianity through Satellite and Radio broadcasts:

In 2015 he was called by the "Sat-7 Pars" Organization to attend an International Education and Development Entity to support the Christians in the Middle East by spreading the Good News of the Kingdom of God through satelite programs as a Televangelist. He completed over 100 Satelite/TV episodes by the end of the 2017. These TV broadcasts are prepared in the Farsi language. To this end, Pastor Edward has travelled to Finland in 2016 and France in 2017 to write and broadcast the episodes for the Good News of the Kingdom of God. In August of 2017, he recorded new Farsi programs from Los Angeles. There is a large Iranian population living in the southern Californis area.

In 2016, National Radio Stations of Finalnd interviewed pastor Edward and he proudly proclaimed his faith and his identity as an Assyrian. He voiced the need for recognition of Assyrian Christians who were persecuated in the Middle East.

Pastor Edward has always been active in the Assyrian community as a respectful pastor and has ministered to the Assyrian community regradless of their denominational differences. He has been invited as a lecturer and speaker in numerous community events and has represented his beloved Assyrian nation and his home church in his community. In addition, in 2015 and 2016 pastor Edward participated in street demostrations in Stanislaus county, Ca, denouncing the Assyrian genocide in the Middle East in the great war of 1914-1918.

Wedding, Edward and Suzanne Eissabake 1995

Eissabake family, Edward, Donton, Suzanne and Daphne 2016

Televangelist office setting, Finland 2016

Presentation of 1928 photo of Assyrian Presbyterian Church, Turlock, CA

Pastor Edward and Martyr

APPENDiX

Celebration Documents

Invitation Letter

ST. JOHN'S ASSYRIAN PRESBYTERIAN CHURCH
EVANGELICAL PRESBYTERIAN CHURCH- EPC
In Essentials Unity, In Non-Essentials Liberty, In All Things Charity

Mailing Address: P.O. BOX 368, Turlock, CA 95381
450 South Palm Street. Turlock, CA 95380
www.stjohnapc.com

July 25th, 2016

Dear St. John Member(s) and Friend(s),

Greetings in the name of our Lord and Savior Jesus Christ!

With great enthusiasm, we would like to inform you that **the Turlock Historical Society has chosen the St. John Assyrian Presbyterian Church as the first Assyrian church of Turlock to be featured in their 2nd annual "How Turlock became the 'City of Churches'" event.**

This will take place on **Tuesday August 2, 2016, at 6:30 pm** in the St. John's main sanctuary.

We hope you can join us to meet Dr. Milton David, son of the founder of the church (the late Rev. Dr. Elisha David), to hear about the 90+ years of the history and amazing work of God in the church and to see the old artifacts and pictures from the past.

We are looking forward to celebrate this wonderful historical event together. God's grace and mercy be upon you.

In His Holy Name,

Rev. *[signature]*

Pastor Edward William Eissabake

"But you are a chosen generation, a royal priesthood, a holy nation, His own special people, that you may proclaim the praises of Him who called you out of darkness into His marvelous light;"(1 Peter 2:9)

The Celebration Program
Front Page

The Turlock Historical Society Proudly Presents Our Second Annual:
How Turlock became the 'City of Churches'
Tuesday, August 2, 2016

St. John's Assyrian Presbyterian Church

The purpose of the Church is to glorify God, to proclaim the Gospel, to cultivate Christ like lives, and to establish love, justice, and peace among all groups of people. And to be the channel of God's saving power, so that His kingdom may come and His will be done in all the earth.

The Presbyterian Church is a Protestant Church and its form is government through elected representatives known as presbyters. Presbyters are ministers and ruling elders, who are equal in the governing bodies of the Church. The ordained officers in a local Presbyterian Church are ministers, ruling elders, and deacons.

The governing bodies of the Presbyterian Church are the Sessions, the Presbytery, and the General Assembly.

St. John's Assyrian Presbyterian Church
Evangelical Presbyterian Church-EPC
In Essentials Unity, In Non-Essentials Liberty,
In All Things Charity
Mailing Address: P.O. BOX 368, Turlock, CA 95381
450 South Palm Street, Turlock, CA 95380

The Celebration Program
Page Two

Turlock Historical Society Second Annual:

How Turlock became the 'City of Churches'

Presenting:

St. John's Assyrian Presbyterian Church

Gathering/Welcome:	Mrs. Monica Boehme
	Turlock Historical Society
Historical Society:	Mrs. Thea Harris
	Turlock Historical Society

A Brief History of the Turlock Assyrian Colony and Arrival of the David Family as the Founder of the Assyrian Presbyterian Church

                      Dr. Milton David
Son of the late Rev. Dr. David Founder and first pastor of the church

The History & Ministry of the 90+ Years of the St. John's Assyrian EPC
                      Rev. Edward William Eissabake
Pastor of the St. John's Assyrian EPC

Presentation of Plaque	Mr. Sam David
	President of Assyrian American Civic Club
Acknowledgment and Closing	Mrs. Monica Boehme
	Turlock Historical Society

Refreshments
Provided by the St. John's Assyrian Presbyterian Church Ladies Group

The Celebration Program
Page Three

St. John's Assyrian Presbyterian Church's Story:

In 1915, while the total population of Turlock reported being 1,300, there were ten Assyrian families living in Turlock. By 1921, the Assyrian community grew to 200 people. The Assyrians migration to the region was so noticeable that the Turlock Daily Journal published an article titled "Assyrian refugees, persecuted by the Turks, are coming to Turlock" (May 14, 1920). On November 10, 1925 the leaders of the worshiping group in an old wooden house (Rev. David Joseph, K.H. Shimmon, Lazar Pera, and George Petros) officially, in writing, extended a call to Rev. Elisha David to organize an Assyrian Presbyterian congregation as Presbyterian was their predominant denomination. To be their pastor, Rev. David came from Dubaque college and seminary in Chicago. Initially, the congregation moved into Swedish Tabernacle, paying rent[1] for the use of it. With the aid of the Board of National Missions-San Francisco (the late Rev. Dr. Philip F. Payne), the Board of New York, and the support of the 4th Presbyterian Church of Chicago (the late Rev. Dr. Timothy Stone) the Assyrian Presbyterian Church as the first Assyrian Church in Turlock[2] and the first only Assyrian registered Presbyterian church west of Chicago[3] was organized by the Presbytery of San Joaquin with almost 60 members on January 13, 1926. On November 27, 1927 the construction of the church building was completed and the church was dedicated by the late Rev. Walter E. Edmunds (from Glendale-Moderator of the Synod of California) on the Sunday morning December 16, 1928[4]. The church was serving San Francisco and Turlock colonies of Assyrian people. The total cost of the church building was $21,000[5]. It came from the donation of the church members, the Assyrian community, and American friends in the United States (California, Chicago and New York). The Architect of the Spanish style building was Rollin S. Tuttle of Oakland, and the builder, Thomas A. Cuthberston from San Francisco. The land was purchased from the City of Turlock for $1,000.

On November 27, 1955, the church adopted the name of the *St. John's* Assyrian Presbyterian Church. In 1958, after joining the Presbyterian USA and United Presbyterian of Northern America, the name of the church was transformed to the St. John's Assyrian *United* Presbyterian Church. In 1983, after joining the United Presbyterian Church and the Presbyterian Church in the U.S., the name of the congregation was called the St. John

The Celebration Ptogram
Page Four

Assyrian Presbyterian Church *(PCUSA)*. The St. John was a member of the Sierra Mission Partnership and the Stockton Presbytery until year 2014 when the St. John's Assyrian PCUSA unanimously voted to join the Evangelical Presbyterian Church *(EPC)* denomination.

Pastors of the St. John's Assyrian EPC and the years of their ministries:

- the late Rev. Dr. Elisha David (D.D.) (1925-1954)
- the late Rev. Stephen O. Khoobyar (1956-1961)
- the late Rev. Darius B. Yohannan (1963-1983)
- Rev. Dr. George Shahaz (1983-2003)
- Rev. Edward William Eissabake (2003-present)

Other Interim Pastors and Associate Pastors:

*Stockton Presbytery Interim Pastors:
Rev. Dr. Harberts; Rev. Frank Humberger, Rev. Lee Heim.

**Assistant Pastors:
Late Rev. J. Prichard Amstus; Rev. Dr. Dan Erickson (People Matter Ministries-Montana); Rev. Dr. Jon Venema (Senior Pastor of Grace Community Church-Visalia, CA)

Footnotes:

1. The Watchman, Church Extension Board Bulletin, No. 454- San Francisco, CA, January 1936. (On 10th anniversary of the St. John's EPC)
2. Stockton Record (Stockton-San Joaquin County)- Friday December 14th, 1928
3. Fresno Bee, Vol. 13, Section-B No. 2148, December 17th, 1928
4. Turlock Tribune- Volume XIX, No. 139, Friday December 14th, 1928
5. Modesto Herald News- December 17th, 1928

Thank You: Dr. Milton David

Thank you to Dr. Milton David, this event could not have taken place without your initial contact with the Historical Society and your willingness to share your family history. Your faith and support of the church is admirable. Thank you also to Rev Edward Eissabake and Mr. Sargon Eddy for your excitement and hard work that made this event so meaningful and successful.

www.ingramcontent.com/pod-product-compliance
Lightning Source LLC
Chambersburg PA
CBHW081825290426
43661CB00125BA/893